THE WESTHILL PROJECT R.E. 5-16

JEWS

2

Maureen Austerberry

Series editors
JOHN RUDGE
GARTH READ
GEOFF TEECE

Jewish consultants
The Centre for the Study of Judaism
and Jewish Christian Relations

Stanley Thornes (Publishers) Ltd

First published in 1990 by:
Stanley Thornes (Publishers) Ltd
Ellenborough House
Wellington Street
CHELTENHAM GL50 1YD
England

Reprinted 1994

British Library Cataloguing in Publication Data
Austerberry, Maureen
    Jews
    2, pupils' bk.
    1. Judaism
    I. Title   II. Series
    296

    ISBN 1–871402–19–0

Typeset by Kalligraphic Design Ltd, Horley, Surrey
Printed and bound in Hong Kong

Contents

Acknowledgements

Two trust funds have contributed in important ways to the production of all
the materials which make up the Jewish strand within the Westhill Project
R.E. 5–16. St Peter's Saltley Trust made a grant to the Regional R.E. Centre
in Westhill College and the Anne Frank Fonds (Switzerland) made a grant
to the Centre for the Study of Judaism and Jewish/Christian Relations in
the Selly Oak Colleges. These two grants enabled Sarah Montagu to share
time between the two Centres. In relation to this project, Sarah has
contributed in the capacity of author and consultant. The authors, editors
and publishers are grateful for these generous grants. They would also like
to thank Rabbi Arye Forta of the Lubavitch Council for Schools and
Rachelle Gryn for their contribution to the content of this book.

The authors and publishers are grateful to the following for permission to
reproduce copyright material in this book:

Photographs

Cover:
Jerry Wooldridge, Juliette Soester.

Inside pages:
Jerry Wooldridge pages 6, 20, 22, 23, 24, 25, 26, 27, 28, 29, 31 (top), 35, 37,
38, 39, 40, 41, 42, 46, 48, 49, 50, 53.
Rex Features page 19.
Juliette Soester pages 30, 31 (bottom), 36, 44, 45, 47, 52.
Robert Hawkins page 43.

Illustrations

Alice Englander pages 5, 21, 51, 57, 58, 59, 60.
Tina Adams pages 7, 8, 32–3, 34.
Edward Ripley pages 9, 10, 11, 12, 13, 14, 15, 16, 17, 18, 26, 27, 34.

Text

The author and publishers are grateful for permission to reproduce extracts
from *Night* by Elie Wiesel, ©Les Editions de Minuit, 1958, published in
Penguin Books, 1981.

1 Jewish community life

Stories

Everyone who can hear and understand words has heard some stories. We can hear stories when people read them to us or we can watch and hear them on the television and radio. We can read stories for ourselves in comics, books or newspapers.

Everyone who can speak has told stories. We can tell stories about things we have done, seen or thought about. We can tell stories about imaginary people, places or creatures.

Some stories are very exciting and may make us feel angry, sad or happy. We often like stories about other people's adventures, or stories which help us to imagine things and places we have never seen. Other stories can make us think about what we would like to do, or perhaps what we would not like to do.

Some stories are about things that happened a long time ago and some are about things that are happening today. Lots of people enjoy reading stories that are about things which might happen in the future.

Perhaps you could talk to your friends about some of your favourite stories. Perhaps you could think about what it might be like to have never heard a story.

Some stories are very old. They have been told many many times over a long period of time. All the religions of the world have these kinds of ancient stories. In this book we will read some ancient stories which are important for Jewish people.

Stories about the beginnings of the Jewish people

Many Jewish people believe in God.

Jews have some very special books about God and the most important of these books is called the Torah. There are lots of stories in the Torah. All of these stories are very ancient and many of them are told again and again by Jews to remind them of what they believe about their community and about God.

In the next few pages you can read three of these stories. One is about how the world began. One is about a man called Abram or Abraham who believed God told him to start a new nation in a new land. The third story is about God giving laws to the Jewish people to guide them on how to live.

Later in this book you will read about many of the things that Jewish people do in their homes and synagogues to express their religious beliefs. You will find that lots of these things reflect different parts of these stories.

God makes the world

In the beginning God created the heavens and the earth.

God said 'Let there be light.' And there was light, God divided the light from the darkness. The light God called day, the darkness God called night. Evening came and morning came; the first day.

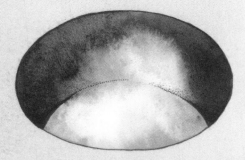

God said, 'Let there be a dome to separate the waters above the dome from the waters on the earth below.' And there was a dome. God called the dome, sky. Evening came and morning came; the second day.

God said, 'Let the waters come together in one place and let the dry land appear.' God called the dry land earth and God called the waters seas. God said, 'Let the earth grow seed-bearing plants and fruit trees.' And it was so. Evening came and morning came; the third day.

God said, 'Let there be lights in the sky marking off day from night.' God made the sun to light the day and the moon and the stars to light the night. Evening came and morning came; the fourth day.

God said, 'Let the waters be full of living creatures and let birds fly above the earth under the sky.' God blessed them and said, 'Be fertile. Let there be great shoals of fish in the seas and great flocks of birds in the sky.' Evening came and morning came; the fifth day.

God said, 'Let there be all sorts of living creatures on the earth, domestic animals, reptiles and wild animals.' God said, 'Let us make people in our image. Let these people be in charge of all other living creatures. Let the people and all other creatures be fertile and multiply, and let them eat the plants and fruit.' And so it was. Evening came and morning came; the sixth day.

When God finished creating everything it was all very good. God rested on the seventh day and blessed that day. It was a holy day because it was the day when all God's work was finished.

God's covenant with the Jewish people

Abram lived a long, long time ago in the city of Haran. The people of Haran worshipped many gods but Abram believed in one God.

One day Abram believed that God was speaking to him. 'Abram, I want you to leave your country and your father's family. Take your wife and go to another land. I will show you the way and tell you when you have arrived there. I promise to make you famous and you will be the founder of a new nation.'

Abram was not told exactly where he had to go or how to get there. He believed that God would show him the way to this new land that he was promised. So he put his trust in God and set out with Sarai, his wife, and his flocks on his adventure into an unknown land.

After many weeks of travelling, Abram and Sarai came to the land of Canaan. While they were camped there, Abram believed that God was speaking to him. 'This is the land that I will give you and to all of your descendants,' said God. 'Abram, look up into the sky and count the stars!'
'There are far too many,' answered Abram. 'I could never count them all.'
'Of course you can't,' said God. 'But one day you will have as many descendants as there are stars in the sky.

Abram and Sarai were surprised to hear this promise from God. How could it ever come true? They did not have any children at all.

Then God said to Abram, 'There are two things that I want you to do to remind you of my promises. These promises are a covenant that I have made with you and your descendants. First, I want you to change your names from Abram and Sarai to Abraham and Sarah. Then I want you to circumcise all men and boys in your family. When you do this, it will remind you that you all belong to me.'

9

Even though Abraham believed that God had told him that Canaan was the place where he was to settle with his family, he had to keep travelling for quite a while. This was because there were many droughts and famines in Canaan and they had to go in search of food. In this search for food they travelled as far as Egypt and back before they eventually settled again in Canaan.

By the time they had settled in Canaan, Abraham had two sons. One was called Ishmael and his mother was Hagar, one of Sarah's slave girls. The other was called Isaac and Sarah was his mother. Abraham's two sons were circumcised to keep the covenant which God had made with Abraham. After a while, Hagar and Ishmael left the family living in Canaan and went to live in another land.

One day Abraham was again sure that God was talking to him. This time he believed that God was telling him to sacrifice his son Isaac.

Abraham was very upset and wondered how this could be, especially if God was to keep his promise of giving Abraham countless numbers of descendants. Still Abraham believed that he must obey God in all things.

Abraham saddled his donkey and took with him two servants and his son Isaac. He chopped wood for the burnt offering and started out for the mountain. When they got to the place on the mountain Abraham said to his servant,
'Stay here with the donkey.
The boy and I will go over there.
We will worship and come back
to you.'

Abraham took the wood and loaded it on Isaac and he himself carried the fire and the knife. Then the two of them set out together. Isaac spoke to his father Abraham. 'Father,' he said. 'Yes, my son.'

'Look,' he said. 'Here are the fire and the wood, but where is the lamb for the burnt offering?'

Abraham answered, 'My son, God will provide the lamb for the burnt offering.'

When they arrived at the place God had pointed out to him, Abraham built an altar there and arranged the wood. Then he bound his son Isaac and put him on the altar on top of the wood. Abraham stretched out his hand and seized the knife to kill his son. Just as Abraham was about to kill his son as a sacrifice, he again heard God speaking to him. 'Abraham, Abraham, do not raise your hand against the boy. Do not harm him for now I know you obey me. You have not refused me your son, your beloved son.'

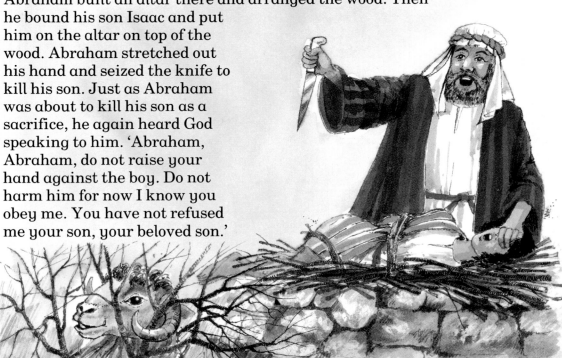

Then Abraham looked up and saw a ram caught by its horns in a bush. Abraham took the ram and offered it as a sacrifice in place of his son.

'You are a very faithful and obedient man, Abraham,' said God. 'You have shown this by your willingness to sacrifice even your son. Because of this I will also bless you and all the descendants I have promised you.' Then they returned home to Sarah and the rest of the family.

God gives the Law to the Jewish people

Many years later there was a famine in Canaan and Abraham's descendants, the Israelites, went to Egypt to look for food. Life in Egypt, with lots of food and work, was so pleasant that the Israelites settled there. They stayed there for a very long time. As the years went by, they greatly increased in number, until there were many thousands of them living in Egypt.

Many generations later, there were so many Israelites that the Egyptians became afraid of them. This made the Egyptians treat them very harshly and turn them all into slaves. The lives of the slaves were made so miserable that many of them cried out to God to set them free.

One day the pharaoh's daughter rescued an Israelite baby from the river. She called him Moses and took him back to the palace and cared for him as though he was her own son. However, even though Moses grew up in the palace surrounded by luxury, he never forgot that he was really an Israelite slave and not an Egyptian prince. One day he saw an Egyptian being terribly cruel to one of the Israelite slaves. He was so angry that he killed the Egyptian. Because of this, Moses had to leave the palace and the country of Egypt and hide in another land.

Some time later, while Moses was caring for some sheep out in the fields he saw a strange thing. In front of him was a bush which was surrounded by fire, but it was not burning. As he went near to the bush he heard a voice telling him to take off his shoes. He knew that this was what people did when they felt near to God.

Then he heard God speaking to him. He believed that God was telling him to go back to Egypt and lead the Israelites out of slavery and to the land God had promised them.

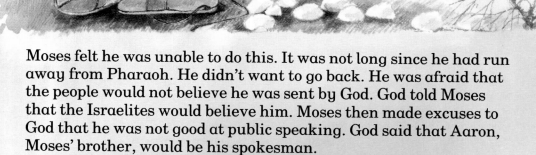

Moses felt he was unable to do this. It was not long since he had run away from Pharaoh. He didn't want to go back. He was afraid that the people would not believe he was sent by God. God told Moses that the Israelites would believe him. Moses then made excuses to God that he was not good at public speaking. God said that Aaron, Moses' brother, would be his spokesman.

At last Moses and Aaron went to the court of Pharaoh. There they pleaded with Pharaoh to let the Israelites go. Pharaoh, the great king who was a god in the eyes of his people, refused. Moses and Aaron warned Pharaoh of the terrible things that would happen if he did not let the Israelites go. Sure enough a series of plagues came to the people of Egypt. The last and most awful plague caused the death of all the first-born children of Egyptian families. Moses had warned the Israelites of this plague. He told them to smear some blood from a lamb on the doorposts of their houses so that this 'angel of death' would pass over their homes. The Israelites did this and their children were saved from the terrible plague. When Pharaoh's eldest son died he was compelled to change his mind and let the Israelites go free.

The Israelites had a hurried meal on that terrible night. They ate roast lamb and bread which looked like flat biscuits. When the meal was finished they quickly packed their belongings and gathered their animals together and began to leave Egypt.

Later the pharaoh regretted his order to let the Israelites go and set out with his chariots and soldiers to recapture his slaves. By the time Moses and the Israelites had reached the Red Sea, Pharaoh and his army were close behind them. The people were afraid that either Pharaoh would capture them or that they would be drowned in the sea. But Moses led his people through it on dry ground caused by a strong east wind sweeping the water back. The Egyptians pounding along behind them on horses were drowned when the sea and wind turned against them. The Israelites felt that God was very near to them and was taking care of them.

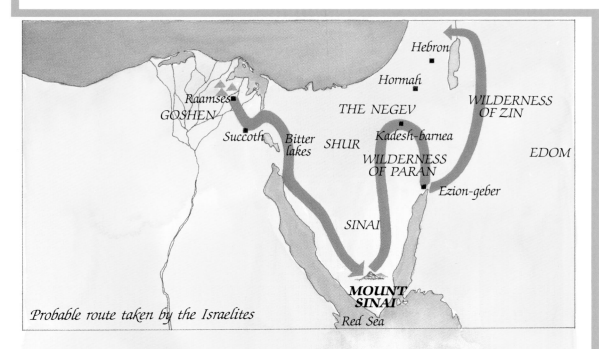

Probable route taken by the Israelites

Not long after the crossing of the Red Sea the Israelites complained to Moses. 'We had good water to drink and lots of food to eat in Egypt. Out here the water is bitter and we have little to eat. Why have you brought us out here in the desert to die?'

Moses asked God what he should do. God said, 'Throw a piece of the wood which I will show you into the bitter water.' Moses threw the wood into the water and the water became sweet.

Then God said, 'Bread will rain down from the sky. The people may gather enough for each day. On the sixth day they must gather enough for two days so that they need not gather food on the seventh day. This bread from heaven is called manna.'

God said, 'A flock of quails will settle near the camp each evening. These you may have as meat.' God said, 'Between dusk and dark you will have flesh to eat and in the morning bread in plenty. You shall know that I am your God.'

One day the people were camped near a large mountain called Sinai. Moses decided that he wanted to be alone with God, so he climbed the mountain by himself.

Once again Moses believed that God was talking to him. 'Moses,' God said, 'tell the Israelites that if they will obey my laws and serve me, they will be my chosen people.'

God then gave Moses a set of ten rules or commandments which were to guide the people in their efforts to serve God and live good lives. These commandments were so important that they were engraved on two large tablets of stone.

While Moses was away on Mount Sinai the people grew tired of waiting for him. They persuaded Moses' brother, Aaron, to help them make a golden calf for them to worship, like other people did.

When Moses came back to the camp with the laws God had given him, he saw the people worshipping the golden calf which they had made. This made him so angry that he smashed the tablets of stone and the calf which the people were worshipping.

Later he returned to the top of the mountain to ask God to forgive the people and give him the ten commandments again. God did this and Moses and the Israelites were able to continue their journey towards the land God had promised them.

Moses made a special container to hold the tablets of stone with the ten commandments engraved on them. This was called the ark and it, with the tablets inside, became a very special reminder to the people that they had agreed to worship God and never again to worship anybody or anything else.

After travelling again for some time the Israelites came near to the land God had promised them. Moses looked out over the land from the top of the mountain and longed to settle with his people in this new place. But this was not to be. He died before the wandering Israelites reached their journey's end. Another leader called Joshua led the people into their promised land.

Festivals

A festival is a celebration of something that is very important. It is important to a whole community and not just to one or two people or families.

Many religious festivals take place at special times each year and help people to express some of their deepest beliefs and commitments.

There are a number of festivals that help Jews to remember special times, events and people that are important to them and their history. These festivals, which are celebrated in many parts of the world, help Jews to know how important each member is to the worldwide Jewish community.

These festivals give Jewish people a chance to enjoy a lot of fun and happiness through feasts, songs, dancing and special rituals as they share together beliefs that are very important to them.

Many of the festivals are linked with stories about the beginnings of the Jewish people. As you read about some of the ways in which Jewish festivals are celebrated today, you should note the ways in which different parts of these stories are retold and at times acted out in rituals.

Shabbat

The most important festival for Jews is Shabbat or the Sabbath. It is a weekly celebration that Jews have been keeping for thousands and thousands of years. For most Jews it is a very holy day and it begins on Friday evening and ends on Saturday evening. It is linked to the stories in the Torah about how God made the world and how God helped the Jewish people escape from slavery and return to their own land. Many of the things that Jews do as part of their celebrations of Shabbat are linked to these two stories.

As you read about four of the ways in which Jews celebrate Shabbat today, see if you can find the parts of the stories which are being remembered through the rituals and other activities.

Many Jews do not work on Shabbat. They believe it is a special day set aside for worship, rest, study and leisure.

They believe that six days are enough each week for hard work and all the other tasks that keep people busy, such as earning a living, tending the garden, buying and cooking food. The seventh day, or Shabbat, is for rest from all that business and a time to celebrate their belief in God, the creator of all life.

There are two special rituals in Jewish homes to help them celebrate Shabbat. One is a welcome to the day on Friday evening and the other is the farewell to Shabbat and a preparation for another week, which takes place on Saturday evening. During the welcome rituals, two candles are lit, a cup of wine shared and two loaves of bread are cut. Usually the mother lights the candles and the father recites the Kiddush or blessings over the bread and wine.

The farewell to Shabbat is marked by the family putting out the flame of a plaited candle in some wine spilled from a very full glass. A box of spice is passed round for all to smell. It is a reminder of the sweetness of Shabbat. Then everyone wishes each other a good week.

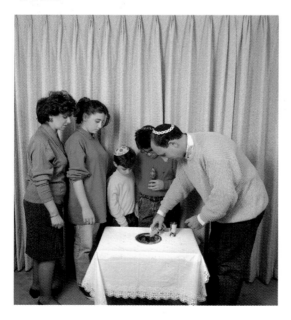

Many Jewish people believe that it is important to go to the synagogue on Shabbat to join in worship with others who are celebrating this weekly festival. One of the important parts of the worship at the synagogue is the opening of the ark where copies of the Torah scrolls are kept. The opening of the ark and the preparation of the scrolls for reading help the worshippers to remember their belief that the Torah contains the record of God's promises to the Jews and the commandments by which they should live.

HEAR O ISRAEL THE LORD OUR GOD THE LORD IS ONE

Another important part of the celebrations of Shabbat for many Jews is to spend time reading and studying the Torah. These people believe that hearing the Torah read during worship at the synagogue is not enough, if they are to understand how God wants them to live. The quiet and restful nature of Shabbat gives them an ideal opportunity for careful reading and study of their holy book at home.

Shabbat is a happy and joyful time because on that day each week Jews believe that they feel God's presence, hear God's promises and learn God's commandments.

Pesah

The Pesah or Passover festival takes place in late March or early April. It lasts for eight days and includes a lot of celebrations in Jewish homes and synagogues.

Again, as you read about several of the things that Jews do during this festival see if you can remember the parts of the stories from the Torah that are being recalled or celebrated.

One very important part of this festival is the celebration of the Seder meal. The meal usually takes place in the home on the first or sometimes the second day of the festival.

Before the meal begins, a special ceremony takes place using a number of different symbolic foods set out on a Seder plate. The word 'seder' means 'order' and these foods are eaten in the special order set out in a book called the Hagaddah.

Perhaps by looking at the names of these foods and what they symbolise, you may work out which of the ancient Jewish stories is being remembered when people eat them during Pesah.

Food	Symbolising
Salt water	the tears of the slaves
Bitter herbs	the hardships of slavery
Haroset	the mortar the slaves used to make bricks
Lamb bone	the lamb killed on the night the slaves escaped from Egypt
Roasted egg	spring and the sacrifices Jewish people made at their ancient temple

During the eight days of this festival Jewish people do not eat any leavened bread. Leavened bread is made with yeast which helps put the air bubbles in the dough. This is what makes the bread rise and become light and fluffy. However, for this to happen, the dough with the yeast in it must be left standing for a while to let the yeast grow.

During Pesah, Jewish people eat only unleavened bread called matzot. This is flat and biscuit-like and can be made quickly. It doesn't have any yeast in it and therefore doesn't need the time to rise.

This eating of unleavened bread also reminds Jews of a part of that same ancient story. Have you found which of the stories it is and which part is being remembered when they eat the unleavened bread?

In the picture you can see a loaf of ordinary leavened bread beside a packet of matzot.

Shavuot

The festival of Shavuot is kept 50 days after the first day of Pesah. This festival recalls the story about Moses on Mount Sinai and how he received from God the Ten Commandments or rules for living.

On this festival day, the Ten Commandments are read during the worship in the synagogue and the congregation stands up in reverence. The synagogues are decorated with flowers and plants.

On the night before the festival many Jews spend all night reading and discussing the Torah. During this night a splendid meal is eaten which includes honey and milky foods. This reminds the Jews of the part in the story when God told Moses what the land to which they were travelling would be like.

The Lord said, 'I have indeed seen the misery of my people in Egypt. I have heard their outcry against their slave-masters. I have taken heed of their sufferings and have come down to rescue them from the power of Egypt, and to bring them out of that country into a fine, broad land; it is a land flowing with milk and honey.'

Exodus 3:7–8

Milk and honey are therefore symbols of the Torah and the promised land. Often honey or sweets are given to a child who is beginning to learn the Torah for the first time.

Sukkot

Sukkot or the festival of the Tabernacles is celebrated in the autumn. It is a joyous occasion which lasts for eight or nine days. It reminds Jews of the time when the Israelites wandered in the wilderness and did not have permanent homes but lived in tents.

Sukkot is also a time when Jews thank God for the harvest. In ancient times people built simple huts in the field to be near their crops, particularly at harvest time. 'Sukkot' is the Hebrew word for huts or booths.

Today Jews build booths or huts at home and at the synagogue for the festival of Sukkot. These are usually built outside or adjoining one of the doors of the house. In any case they are arranged so that the stars can be seen through their roofs. Meals are eaten in them and some people even sleep in them.

During the morning service at the synagogue, four plants are waved in all directions. These plants are the palm, the myrtle, the willow and a yellow citrus fruit called an etrog.

Here is a little puzzle for you. It is based on one idea that Jews have about why the four species or plants are used in the rituals of Sukkot.

Using the old Jewish saying in dark type and the descriptions of each species, work out your ideas about what this symbolic act might be saying about the Jewish community.

'Taste represents learning and smell represents good deeds.'

The palm has taste but no smell.   The myrtle has smell but no taste.

The citrus has taste and smell.   The willow has no smell and no taste.

The last day of the festival of Sukkot is called Simhat Torah. The word 'simhat' is the Hebrew word for rejoicing. This is a time when the Jews rejoice that God has given them the commandments and taught them about how to live a good life.

Jewish people read a part of the Torah in their synagogue each week. These readings are arranged so that it takes exactly one year to read the whole of the Torah.

This yearly cycle of reading the Torah is completed on Simhat Torah and a new one started. On this day, every scroll of the Torah is taken out of the ark and carried round the synagogue in procession. It is a joyful occasion and many people dance, clap or sing while the scrolls are paraded around the synagogue. Some people dance with the scroll in their arms to show how much they love God's commandments.

In some synagogues the women in the gallery throw sweets to the children who may be downstairs joining in the dancing with the men.

The festivals of Pesah, Shavuot and Sukkot are called the pilgrim festivals and are linked to stories in the Torah. They are called pilgrim festivals because in ancient times as many Jews as possible would travel to their capital city, Jerusalem, to join in these very special festivals.

Purim

This festival is based on a story about a Jewish queen called Esther who lived a long time ago. She too helped her people to escape from some terrible persecutions. One of the highlights of this festival is the reading of the story in the synagogue. The story is read from the scroll of Esther, which is folded to look like the letter Queen Esther sent to the Jews. Whenever the name of Haman, the enemy of the Jews, is mentioned, the congregation shout, stamp, boo and make such a noise that his name is blotted out. The children are encouraged to make as much noise as possible. To help them do this they take whistles and rattles along to the synagogue. There are special Purim prayers said for that day.

Often after the service there is a special tea with Purim cakes that are triangular in shape, which some Jews call 'Haman's ears' and other Jews call 'Haman's pockets'. Sometimes there is a fancy dress parade or a play about the story of Queen Esther to entertain the congregation.

Purim is also a time for sending gifts to friends and relations and giving money to charities. Some Jewish people also go without food for one day before the festival begins.

As you read this story of Queen Esther see if you can find out why the festival is called Purim. You may also find the reason why some Jews fast before the festival begins.

The story of Queen Esther

Esther was a Jewish girl who lived a long time ago in Persia, or Iran as it is called today. She was a very beautiful girl and one day the king of Persia chose her to be his queen though he did not know at the time that she was Jewish.

The Persian king, Xerxes, had a chief minister called Haman. He was a very powerful man and very proud. He made everyone bow down and worship him. If they didn't, he would have them killed. Queen Esther's uncle Mordecai refused to bow to Haman because Mordecai was a Jew and he said that Jews only bow down to God. Haman plotted to kill Mordecai and all other Jews who would not bow down to him. He drew lots (purim) to find a date when the Jews would be killed. A date was fixed.

When Queen Esther heard about this she wondered how she could save her uncle and all her people. She sent a message to the Jews telling them to fast for three days. She and her maids did the same. Then she prepared two banquets for the king and Haman.

In those days, the queen was not allowed to see the king unless he sent for her. However, Esther decided that she must break this rule and act quickly if her people were to be saved. She also realised that because of her actions it would be known that she belonged to the Jewish community. Esther was very relieved when the king saw her and agreed to come to her banquets.

After the first banquet the king could not sleep. To entertain him, one of his court officials read some of the royal records to him. Listening to these he heard how Mordecai, the Jew, had once saved his life. So he decided that on the next day he would find a way to honour Mordecai.

At the second banquet Esther told the king about Haman's wickedness. The king was so angry that Haman was plotting to kill the man who had saved him that he ordered that Haman should be killed and Mordecai made minister in his place. Because of Esther's brave actions all the Jewish people were saved from the death that Haman had planned for them.

Rosh haShanah

At the beginning of the Jewish New Year, which happens sometime in September or October, Jews celebrate the festival of Rosh haShanah. These Hebrew words mean 'the head of the year'.

This festival is also linked to three of the ancient stories found in the Torah.

God makes the world

In Jewish tradition, Rosh haShanah is the day on which God started creating the world. Sometimes this day is referred to as 'the birthday of the world'. So it not only marks the beginning of the Jewish New Year, it also reminds Jews of their belief that God created the whole world and all people. When the Jewish people share some apple dipped in honey at the Kiddush after the synagogue worship on this day they are looking back to the creation of the world and looking forward to a sweet and happy new year.

Abraham obeys God

Rosh haShanah is also a time when Jews remember their belief that all people should obey God. This is why the telling of the story of Abraham obeying God is an important part of the celebration. The blowing of the ram's horn or shofar during the festival recalls the way in which Abraham sacrificed a ram instead of his son.

God gives the Law to the Jewish people

Rosh haShanah also reminds Jews of their belief that the Torah is the record of the laws which God gave to Moses such a long time ago. Many Jews believe that when Moses received these laws on Mount Sinai people could hear the sound of the blowing of the shofar.

Rosh haShanah reminds Jews of their belief that they belong to God, and that they must obey the laws which God has given to them. They are also reminded of the ways in which they have failed to do this. So this day is also a time for being sorry and for seeking God's forgiveness for all their past mistakes.

Yom Kippur

Rosh haShanah is a time for remembering and being sorry for past sins and mistakes. Ten days after Rosh haShanah Jews celebrate another very solemn day called the Day of Atonement or Yom Kippur. On this day they try to make amends for their sins and receive God's forgiveness.

Many people stay at the synagogue throughout the whole of this day. In most synagogues there will be five different services of prayer and readings from the Torah. Most of the decorations, flowers and the ark coverings in the synagogue are likely to be white and many of the worshippers will be dressed in white. Fasting, that is going without food or drink, will also be an important part of the day for many people. Many synagogues also take a collection of money for charity during the days before this time of repentance and forgiveness.

Three important Jewish beliefs about repentance for sins are expressed in the activities of Yom Kippur.

- *Confession.* Jewish people believe that all people make mistakes and at times hurt themselves and others. Owning up or confessing to this is an important thing for people to do.

- *Sorrow.* Many of the prayers and readings in the synagogue on Yom Kippur help Jews to express how sorry they are for all their mistakes.

- *Amends.* Yom Kippur is also a time when Jews are encouraged to make amends for the hurt they may have caused others by their sin.

The final service in the synagogue on Yom Kippur ends with the congregation joining in the recitation of three short statements of Jewish belief in one God.

Hear, O Israel: the Lord is our God, the Lord is One.

Blessed be the Lord's name whose glorious kingdom is for ever and ever.

The Lord, the Lord is God.

Then one long note is sounded on the shofar.

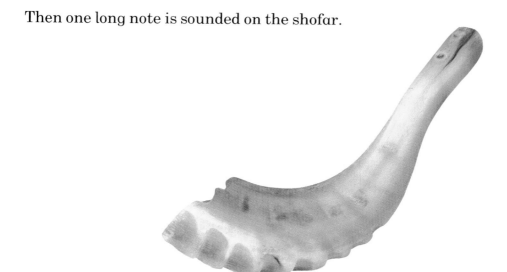

The synagogue

The word 'synagogue' is a Greek word which means 'meeting place'. Most Jews throughout the world call the place where they meet for worship by this name, though some use the word 'temple'.

All Jews use three other Hebrew terms to describe what they see as the main purposes of their synagogue.

- Bet Tefillah (the house of prayer)
- Bet Knesset (the house of meeting)
- Bet Midrash (the house of study)

Rabbi Rachel tells us about her synagogue:

'We meet here for services. During the services we pray, we sing songs, and we study some of the teachings of Judaism. The most important study we do during the service is when we take out the Torah scrolls. They contain the first five books of the Bible, written out very carefully by hand. Some of the members of the synagogue come to help in the reading each week and this is a great honour for them. They say a blessing and then I read from the scroll, a different chapter each week. I have to concentrate very hard when I do this to make sure I don't make any mistakes. First I read the Hebrew, then I translate it into English and then I explain the meaning.

Rabbis don't have any special uniform to wear. Some rabbis do wear robes for services, but I prefer just to wear a tallit or prayer shawl over my usual clothes.

This is a Progressive synagogue, so families sit together during the service. When I was small, I used to join in the songs and then if I didn't understand all the prayers and readings I used to plait up the fringes of my father's prayer shawl. As I grew older, and learnt more Hebrew, I could understand and join in all of the service. When I decided that I wanted to be a rabbi it was still unusual for women to do that, but now there are an increasing number of women who are rabbis or learning to be rabbis.

After the services we go to another room. There we say blessings over wine and bread and have a chance to chat with each other. The children, who had to try to be quiet during the service, help us by taking bread and cake to everyone. Then they can run around and play together.

During the week lots of things happen in the synagogue building. There are classes for children and for adults. There is a mother and toddler group and youth groups for children of all ages and groups for old people. Some of the time I work here in the synagogue, teaching and talking to people. Sometimes I go to visit people in hospitals or at home, or go to meetings. I often talk to Christians and other groups who want to learn more about Judaism.'

Prayer

Praying to God is a very important part of the services which take place at the synagogue, especially on Shabbat. Most of these prayers are read or sung from the Siddur or prayer book. On some occasions, worshippers in the synagogue may have short periods of silence during which they can offer their own very personal, private prayers. Some people shut or cover their eyes during the recitation of the Shema ('Hear, O Israel: the Lord is our God, the Lord is One.'), to help them concentrate on their belief in one God, who listens to and receives all of their prayers.

There are three main kinds of prayers which Jews offer to God during their worship.

- In their prayers of praise, they acknowledge the greatness and holiness of God.
- In prayers of thanksgiving, they are saying how grateful they are for all of the good gifts which God has given to them.
- When they offer prayers of petition, they are asking God for help and guidance for themselves and other people.

Meeting

Most Jewish communities have a special time for meeting each other after their worship at the synagogue. This meeting is called Kiddush, which is the name for a special blessing for the Shabbat. This blessing is said over a cup of wine either at the end of the Friday evening service or after the morning service on Saturday.

After the service, the congregation is invited to Kiddush which is usually held in a hall. Some verses from the Torah which tell about keeping Shabbat are sung. Then a blessing is said or sung over the wine and everyone has a drink. Cakes and biscuits are handed round with the wine. It is an opportunity for members of the congregation to talk and welcome visitors. Sometimes the wine and cakes are provided by one of the families who may be celebrating a special event, such as the birth of a baby.

For many Jews the synagogue is also a place where they meet on several occasions during the week. They may meet in social or educational groups. They may just drop in for a chat or to receive help and advice from the rabbi on all kinds of personal and family issues.

Reading and studying the Torah

The Torah is the Jews' special book about God. The word 'Torah' means 'teaching'. The five books of the Torah are called: Genesis, Exodus, Leviticus, Numbers and Deuteronomy. Because the story of Moses is the most important part of these books Jews call them the 'Five Books of Moses' and many Jews believe that Moses wrote these books.

The copies of the Torah in the synagogue are handwritten by people called scribes. They are written in the Hebrew language. Hebrew is spoken by most people who live in Israel and it is used in synagogues all over the world.

The scrolls have beautiful coverings or mantles and are kept in the ark. The ark is a kind of cupboard on the wall facing Jerusalem. The ark usually has a curtain over its doors.

Parts of the Torah are read in the synagogue each week. These readings are arranged so that the whole of the Five Books of Moses are read through the year.

Most synagogues also have a busy educational programme for children, young people and adults. The study of Torah and of other aspects of Jewish life is an important feature of these programmes.

2   Jewish family life

Marriage

Most people find it lonely to live on their own. They prefer to live with someone else. Most people wish to love and to be loved. When a man and a woman love each other very much they may wish to get married. This is the way most new families begin.

In most communities the beginning of a new family through marriage is usually celebrated with special ceremonies and customs.

Some of these ceremonies are rich in colourful and elaborate rituals. Some are very simple and plain. Some involve large numbers of people and include times for feasting, singing and dancing. Some are very private, involving just the couple being married and a few close relatives and friends.

Wedding ceremonies can take place in many different places. Some are held in the open air, some are held in a registry office and many are held in religious places of worship.

The rituals and ceremonies of religious weddings are usually designed to express strongly held beliefs about marriage. These rituals are likely to be based on very old traditions and will include prayer, readings from several books and hymns or songs.

Jewish weddings

Jewish weddings can take place out in the open, at home or in the synagogue. Most Jewish weddings in Britain take place in the synagogue.

On the Shabbat before the wedding the bridegroom may be called up to read from the Torah. Afterwards many of the peope call out 'mazal tov', which in English means 'good luck'. In some synagogues many people throw raisins or sweets over the groom as an expression of good wishes.

It is the custom for some couples to fast during the day of the wedding until after the ceremony is over. This also helps to show how important the day is and to increase the enjoyment of celebrating the beginning of a new family.

On the day of the wedding the bride and her attendants wait in a special room in the synagogue. The groom and his attendants visit this room and the groom recites the following blessing to his bride. 'Our sister, may you become [the mother of] thousands of ten thousands.' He then covers her face with a veil which remains over her face until the end of the ceremony.

Jewish couples get married while standing under a canopy or huppah. Some of these huppahs are specially made for the occasion. They may be made of a strong wooden frame with a richly embroidered cloth stretched over the top. They will often be decorated with lots of flowers and other greenery. These colourful huppahs are especially popular when the wedding is held in the open air.

Some couples prefer to have a simple tallit or prayer shawl held above them by four friends or other members of the Jewish community.

There are different ideas about why the huppah is used and what it symbolises. Some Jews say that because it is often open to the sky it reminds them that God promised Abraham that his descendants would be as numerous as the stars in the sky.

Others say that it is a reminder of the tent which was specially set aside in ancient times for new brides and grooms. Others say that it symbolises the new home which the couple are about to begin together.

When the marriage ceremony begins, the groom's father and future father-in-law lead the groom to the huppah. The bride's mother and future mother-in-law lead the bride to stand under the huppah with the groom. At least two other adults who will act as witnesses stand beside the couple.

Generally the rabbi conducts the service which begins with him reciting two blessings. Then a cup of wine is shared by the bride and groom.

The groom places a gold ring on the index finger of the bride's right hand and says, 'Behold you are betrothed to me with this ring, according to the law of Moses and of Israel.' The bride's acceptance of the ring shows her consent to the marriage.

Next, the ketuba, or marriage document, is read aloud. This document reminds the couple of their responsibilities towards each other. It is signed by the two witnesses, thus making it a legal document. The bride keeps the ketuba, as proof of her marriage.

Seven blessings are chanted over a second cup of wine, which is then shared by the bride and groom. The recitation of these blessings requires the presence of a minyan or 10 adult male Jews. These blessings sum up the ceremony.

One of the seven marriage blessings

Bring great rejoicing on these loving companions as you brought rejoicing on your first creation in the garden of Eden. Blessed are you, O Lord, who brings rejoicing to bridegroom and bride.

Finally the groom breaks a wine glass, wrapped in a cloth, beneath his foot. Again the origins of this are uncertain. Some say it symbolises the destruction by the Romans of the Temple in Jerusalem nearly 2000 years ago. Others say that this breaking of the glass reminds them that married life can have its misfortunes as well as its joys and the bride and groom must stand together, as they are doing now under the huppah.

After the ceremony, the bride and groom go to a room by themselves for a short time. Here those couples who have fasted before their wedding eat a little food.

A festive meal follows the ceremony and the guests enjoy a time of music and dancing.

Children in Jewish families

Anybody whose mother is Jewish is automatically a member of the Jewish community.

In most cases Jewish parents consider each child to be a blessing and a gift from God. They also believe that it is important that their children grow up knowing what it means to be Jewish. To help them do this they have some important ceremonies at different times in the child's life.

Circumcision

On the eighth day after a boy is born he is circumcised. Circumcision means to cut off the skin around the end of the penis. If the baby is sick or not very strong then the ceremony takes place later.

The Jewish name for this ritual is Brit Milah. In English it means 'Covenant of Circumcision'. You may remember that in the story of Abraham, when God made an agreement or covenant with Abraham, one of the things Abraham was to do to remind him and all Jews of this agreement was to circumcise all male children.

When only eight days old, the baby is brought into the room by his mother. She usually hands the baby to a close female relation or friend, who, in turn, gives the baby to the father. After saying a blessing the

father places the baby on a symbolic chair. The empty chair reminds Jews of Elijah, one of their famous prophets. Many Jews believe that Elijah is present in spirit at this ceremony to ensure that all Jews keep the commandments of God. The baby is then placed in the lap of his godfather or sandek. The sandek holds the baby carefully during the circumcision which is performed by someone called the mohel.

At the end of the Brit Milah the baby is wished a happy and healthy life, as everybody present joins in reciting the following words. 'Just as he has entered the covenant, so may he also enter into the blessings of Torah, of marriage and of good deeds.'

Naming

Names are very important. They are as much a part of us as our head, arms and legs. They help to tell people who we are. This is why Jewish people choose the names of their children very carefully. Nearly all Jewish children have names which are the same as important or well-known people in Jewish history. Having these Hebrew names helps the children and others to know that they belong to the Jewish community.

Here are some names which are very popular with all Jewish families.

Girls: Sarah, Rachel, Ruth, Deborah, Esther
Boys: Daniel, Simon, Michael, Samuel, David, Joseph

Boys are usually given their names at their Brit Milah. A girl's name is usually announced in the synagogue on the Shabbat following the day she is born.

Many synagogues have services of thanksgiving and dedication for boys and girls where parents can express their thanks to God and invite other members of the community to share in their joy. This often includes a special Kiddush after the worship.

Bat/Bar Mitzvah

Jewish children are recognised as 'adult' members of the community at a relatively early age. Girls are treated as full members of the community at age 12 and boys when they are 13. When children reach these ages they are given special titles which acknowledge that they are now members of the Jewish community in their own right.

Girls: Bat Mitzvah (daughter of the Commandment)
Boys: Bar Mitzvah (son of the Commandment)

As soon as possible after their 12th and 13th birthday, usually on the next Shabbat, these young people may read from the Torah, make a small speech about Jewish belief or just give a word of thanks and join in a party to celebrate the event.

Jewish food laws

Many Jewish families believe that preparing and eating food in a Jewish way helps them to remember and keep their identity as Jews. Eating in a Jewish way also shows how Jews are different from, though not necessarily better than, other people.

The laws about what Jews may eat and what they may not eat are based on the Book of Leviticus in the Torah. These laws are called kashrut and the foods which are considered fit for Jews to eat are called kasher foods.

The laws of kashrut have little, if anything to do with ideas about health or hygiene. Jews, like most other people, depend on scientists and doctors to guide them on matters of healthy eating. Jewish people keep these laws because they believe that God commanded them to eat only certain foods.

The rules of kashrut can be divided into three main groups.

Kasher foods

The first group of rules are about what foods are considered to be kasher by Jews:

- all plants, fruits and vegetables
- mammals with split hooves and which chew the cud
- fish with both scales and fins
- all domestic birds
- the milk of any kasher mammal
- the eggs of any kasher bird.

See if you can use these rules to decide which of the things and animals shown in this collage are kasher and which are not.

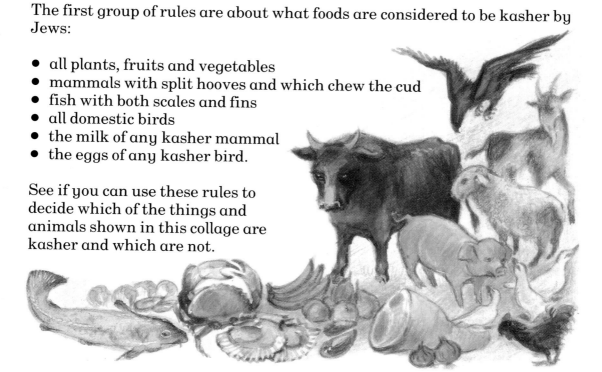

Ritual slaughter (shehitah)

The second set of kashrut rules deals with the killing of animals for food.

Jews kill or slaughter animals for food in what they believe to be the most humane way. The emphasis is on causing the animals the least possible pain and distress. The person trained to do this is called a shohet. This person must also be trained in animal anatomy and Jewish law.

Jews believe that the 'spirit of life' is contained in the blood of all creatures and so they drain all blood from meat before it is eaten. The salting and soaking of meat also helps to remove the blood.

Meat and milk

Jewish kashrut rules also included three restrictions about the way in which meat and milk are used.

- Meat and milk must not be cooked together.
- Meat products and milk products must not be eaten together.
- Meat and milk products must not be used together.

In many Orthodox Jewish homes there are separate sets of cooking utensils, cutlery and cloths to be used when the meal includes either meat or milk products. There are different opinions among Jewish families about the period of time that should be left between eating meat and then eating any milk products. However, most Jews leave about three hours between the eating of these different foods.

3   Jewish personal life

Individuals

We are all unique. There are no two people exactly alike in the whole world. We are all individuals who have to live our own personal lives.

We all have our own likes and dislikes, hopes and fears. We all have our own ideas about what we want to do and what we want to be.

At the same time each of us shares many things in common with all other people. We all share life on this planet as members of the human race. We have the same needs for food and shelter. We all need love, friendship and care from other people. We all experience sickness and suffering and eventually we all die.

We all belong to different groups of people. The groups we belong to also help to form our own personal uniqueness. The race we belong to helps to form the shape, size and colour of our bodies. The families we belong to give us our names and help us to form ideas about how to live.

Perhaps you can think of some more things that are unique to you, and others which you share in common with other people.

In this book we have been reading about Jewish communities and families. For the individual men and women, girls and boys who belong to these communities, being Jewish is very important. It helps them to live in ways which, in many respects, are different from the ways in which other people live. Being a Jew is a special part of the personal identity.

However, this doesn't mean that they don't share many things in common with all other people.

Many years ago, a famous English writer called William Shakespeare wrote a play called *The Merchant of Venice*. At one point in the play a Jewish man called Shylock makes a speech to remind everyone that all people, whatever their race, nationality or religion, share common experiences and feelings with all other people.

As you read part of Shylock's speech, see if you can think of any occasion or situation when you might want to say things like this about yourself and the way other people may be treating you.

> I am a Jew. Hath not a Jew eyes? Hath not a Jew hands, organs, dimensions, senses, affections, passions? Fed with the same food, hurt with the same weapons, subject to the same diseases, healed by the same means, warmed and cooled by the same winter and summer . . .? If you prick us, do we not bleed? If you tickle us, do we not laugh? If you poison us, do we not die?
>
> *The Merchant of Venice*, III, 1

In the next few pages there are stories about individual Jews. One story is about a woman who lived hundreds of years ago and her name was Dona Gracia. The story of Elie Wiesel tells part of the sad story of millions of Jews who were killed in Germany during the World War of 1939–1945. The fourth story is about a Jewish woman living in Britain today.

As you read these stories see if you can pick out those things that make these people Jewish and those which they share in common with all people.

'Then the nightmare began of trying to stay with Father, of obtaining what little food and water there was to eat and drink, the agony endured one day of having to stand all day with one's feet in the mud, the fear that if one fell ill the hospital was not always a place of healing, but of painful experiment. Dentists searched for those with gold and silver fillings. Then there was the deep humiliation of being number A-7713, not a person with a name. A number of us were made to witness the hangings of innocent people, including that of a child. I was beaten a number of times.

'The summer was coming to an end. The Jewish year was nearly over. On the eve of Rosh haShanah, the whole camp was electric with tension – the last day of the year, with the emphasis on last. Our evening meal was a very thick soup, but no one touched it. We wanted to wait until after prayers. Time and again I questioned God who allowed these dreadful things to happen to his people. I felt terribly alone in the world without God and without man, without love or mercy. I couldn't even wish Father a Happy New Year.

'Then came the day when we were taken to another camp, Buchenwald. We were force-marched in an icy wind and snowstorms. Many fell on the way and did not get up again. We arrived at the barracks before getting on the train. It was greatly overcrowded. Juliek, a Polish Jew whom I had not met before, played his violin. He played a fragment from a Beethoven concerto. I had never heard sounds so pure. Afterwards there was such a silence.

'In January 1945 Father fell ill. He lay dying for many days. I was torn between caring for him and trying to remain alive myself. My father died on 28th January. I was now on my own until 11th April when all of us were released. The first act of free men was to find food. We thought of food, not of revenge, not of our families, nothing but bread.'

After the war Elie moved to Paris, where he learned to speak French and took French nationality. His work as a journalist led him to Israel and finally to the USA where he settled with his wife and family.

Eve Silver

Eve Silver is a member of one of Birmingham's synagogues. She was born 45 years ago into a large and close family. Her father had a small shop and at the time when she was born he was trying to build up his business again after all the changes and upheaval of the Second World War. She remembers that things were: 'often hard for the family, but we kept each other company and played together.'

Her parents were members of a synagogue but were not very religious: 'We lit candles on Friday night, went to shul on Rosh haShanah and Yom Kippur but not much more than that.'

When Eve went to college to train as a teacher, she decided she wanted to be more involved with the Jewish religion. She went to Israel for six months when she finished her course: 'It was just the time of the Six Day War (1967). It was a very exciting time to be there, to feel part of what the Jewish people had achieved and to see our ancient country coming to life again.'

When she came back to England, she married Ray Silver whom she had met at college. Ray works for a firm of computer programmers in Birmingham and they both belong to a small Orthodox synagogue. Eve gave up her job as a teacher to look after her three young children, but once they were a bit older she went back to work part-time and then full-time. She also finds time to work for the synagogue Ladies' Guild, which does a lot of fund-raising for charities as well as organising social events for the community. She's just joined a Jewish choir, a group which sings Jewish and other songs in concerts all round Birmingham: 'My first concert with the group is next week. I'm looking forward to it but I'm a bit nervous at the same time.'

Eve's children, Jeremy aged 20, Deborah aged 18 and Jonathan aged 15 are all involved in the community in different ways: 'Jeremy's away at college at the moment. He took a year out between school and university to study at a yeshivah, a religious college, in Israel. He found it quite hard to come back to the 'real world' but he seems more settled now. Deborah's just surprised us all by deciding to join the police force. She says she wants to do something for the whole community, not just the Jewish community. I think she'll find it strange to be the only Jewish person in her group, but I am glad she's found something she wants to do.'

Jonathan's still at school. Eve says of him: 'He's the only one who's taken after his father. Jon lives and breathes computers. As soon as he's home from school, he's upstairs on the computer. In fact, we had a bit of a row recently with him because he wanted to use his computer on Shabbat. We don't use electrical things, like the phone, the TV or a computer, on Shabbat. Jon couldn't get through 25 hours without a computer so we reached a compromise: on Shabbat he is not allowed to use the computer downstairs in the lounge, but what he does in his own room is up to him. He's old enough to make his own decisions about what he does. Last Shabbat we hardly saw him downstairs! I hope this will change soon, but realistically I know it may not. At least he spent an evening recently showing the Jewish Cub Scout group some of his computer games and he seemed to enjoy doing that.'

Eve likes the community here: 'If you're Jewish it sometimes seems that everything Jewish happens in London. This community is quite small – there are only about 2000 Jews in Birmingham – but it's very friendly and there's a lot going on. We may decide to go to Israel to live once all the children have finished their studies and have settled down, but for now we're very happy here.'

Notes for teachers

The material in this book is intended to help children learn about Jews. Jewish practices and beliefs are described clearly and without any assumptions being made about any teacher's or pupil's acceptance of the Jewish religion now or in the future.

Clearly one book cannot deal with every aspect of Judaism. This book, along with others in the set, points to important features of Judaism and gives pupils some clear guidelines for continuing their exploration of this religion.

This book is the second in a set of four books. This one is intended for use with pupils aged 9–11 years. It is therefore best suited for use with pupils in the upper primary school.

There are three parts to the book. Part One extends pupils' understanding of important features of Jewish communities by relating them to important Jewish stories. In fact, the significance and role of story in religion is a dominant theme in this book. Part Two focuses on aspects of Jewish family life. In Part Three pupils are introduced to stories which help them to explore ways in which the Jewish faith is applied by some individual Jews within their own personal lives. The three parts are indicated by colour coding: pink for Part One, blue for Part Two, yellow for Part Three. The coloured box round each page number indicates which part the page is in.

Because this book is part of a structured and developmental scheme, some knowledge of Judaism is assumed. However, some teachers may decide that a particular group of pupils does not have this assumed knowledge and is therefore not ready to proceed with this book. They may well decide that at least some preparatory work, using Book 1 in this set, is necessary.

Content overview of the pupils' books

The four pupils' books in this series are designed to help pupils develop an understanding of Judaism as a world religion. Each book deals with different aspects of Jewish practices, beliefs and experiences.

The diagrammatic presentation below indicates the content of each book and shows how the children are helped to build up, in a progressive way from age 7 to 16 their knowledge and understanding of this religion. The shaded areas in the circles indicate the aspects of Judaism dealt with in particular books.

A more detailed explanation of this way of distributing the materials across the four books is given in the teacher's books, ***How do I teach R.E.?*** and ***Judaism***.

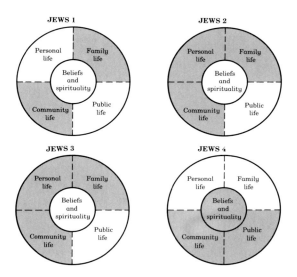

Other materials in this Project

Teachers using this book with upper primary pupils must realise that it is only one resource item designed to meet one specific aspect of the pupils' experience of R.E. – learning about Jews. To expand the range of classroom activities designed to meet this need, a **photopack**, with additional pictures and information, is also available.

Teachers using these classroom resources are strongly recommended to refer to the two teacher's books:

How do I teach R.E.? – the main Project manual.

Judaism – a source book and guide to the teaching of this religion.

Books and photopacks belonging to other religious traditions and various Life Themes are also part of **The Westhill Project R.E. 5–16**.